D0804689

HOW TO HANDLE

TROUBLE

God's Way

By Jay E. Adams

Presbyterian and Reformed Publishing Co.
Phillipsburg, New Jersey 08865

ISBN: 0-87552-076-6

Third printing, December 1986

Printed in the United States of America

All New Testament quotations are from
The Christian Counselor's New Testament.

CONTENTS

PREFACE

This book is written for Christians who find, or will soon find, themselves in trouble. It is for church classes and other groups who wish to study what the Bible says about trouble. In short, it is for every believer. There is no one who does not face trouble—frequently.

How to Handle Trouble, as its title indicates, is not merely a biblical study of the subject; it is a practical handbook that gives biblical directions to follow in times of trouble.

It is my earnest desire to see our Lord Jesus Christ exalted more fully in your life as a result of following the biblical guidelines set forth in this book.

Blessings!

Jay E. Adams
The Millhouse, 1981

INTRODUCTION

Are you in trouble? Chances are that if you have picked up this book either you or someone you know is. If so, this is the book for you.

Maybe you've just emerged from some trouble. How did you handle it? Did you whine ("Why?" "Why this?" "Why me?" "Why now?"); did you become angry or resentful; did you go all to pieces? If so, this book is for you.

Has it been some time since you have been in trouble? Well then, look out! Trouble may be waiting for you just around the next corner! Do you want to know what to do when it comes, how to prepare for it, and what to do if you cannot avoid it? Then this is the book for you.

Trouble! We all face it—often. How important it is, then, to understand trouble and know what to do when it comes!

WHAT TROUBLE IS

Everyone experiences trouble, and everyone can identify it when it comes; but not everyone *understands* it. The English word *trouble* comes from a root that means turbid, agitated, disturbed, stirred up, and upset, indicating the principal factors involved in trouble. The idea is that circum-

1

stances (and often, as a result, your own equilibrium) are stirred up by trouble. Trouble somehow changes things for the worse and irritates you, usually in a way that puts pressure on you to respond. While that element of response is not clearly found as the focus of any of the biblical root terms for trouble, nevertheless the idea of involvement inherent in each and reflected in our expression "to *face* trouble" implies pressure to make a response. And, as you know, this very *demand* for a response is often the most difficult fact about trouble.

CHRISTIANS IN TROUBLE

This book is written to Christians. Christians know why there is trouble in God's world. It is not because of the way the world was created. God created it trouble-free. All the trouble in the world ultimately comes from Adam's sin. It was Adam's fall into sin that brought about God's curse on the world. That's when trouble began: trouble with God, with one's fellow man, and with the world itself. Moreover, you and I, as sinful sons of Adam, make more trouble for ourselves and others because *we* sin. Trouble is a constant reminder of sin and the curse.

Christians, however, are people whose sins have been forgiven. That means two things: (1) By the death and resurrection of Jesus Christ Christians have been saved from hell, the final, eternal and worst trouble of all. (2) They have been given a new nature capable of understanding and handling trouble in ways an unbeliever cannot, as long as they do so God's way.

While God has not yet removed trouble from the Christian or the Christian from trouble[1] (indeed, becoming a Christian means taking on a whole new set of troubles[2]), He has, by the Word and His Spirit, given believers all that is necessary to handle trouble successfully.

If you are a Christian, this book is for you. But if you are not, I want you to understand that its biblical promises are not for you. They can be yours only if you trust Christ as your Savior. If you have never acknowledged your sin as an offense against a holy God whose commandments you have broken, then you must do so. If, indeed, you are sorry for your sin, tell Him so, ask His forgiveness, and believe in Jesus Christ as your Savior.

It will do no good to go through the motions or say the right words as a gimmick to get out of trouble; you must *mean* what you say. You can deceive others, but you cannot deceive God; He knows your heart. I suggest that you read the Gospel of John several times, noting the emphasis on *belief*. If you truly believe that Jesus died in your place, taking the punishment you deserve for your sins, you will be saved from hell and will find a new life here and now. All who trust Him find forgiveness and eternal life.

1. That will happen only in eternity (Rev. 21:4).
2. While it is true that living the Christian life precludes many self-inflicted troubles, it also brings persecution from others (II Tim. 3:12).

3

If you are already a Christian or have trusted Christ as a result of what you have just read, you are entitled to the promises of God that pertain to trouble. But one final word of warning: salvation from sin and its consequences is a matter of faith in the Christ who came, not merely to help you in trouble, but to change your entire life. Salvation is not something you *add* to what you were before you became a Christian. It is something that saves you from your former patterns of life. Salvation means that you handle trouble God's way *instead of* the ways you have handled it in the past. Christ and pagan ways do not mix. If you trust Him, He transforms your whole perspective on life.

SOME BIBLICAL TERMS FOR TROUBLE

Wilson's *Old Testament Word Studies* lists 30 biblical Hebrew words that have been translated "trouble." How much trouble there is that it would take 30 words to express it! Obviously, it would not be helpful to discuss each one here. It will be enough, perhaps, to note the great attention the Scriptures pay to the topic and then to look more carefully at the three most significant terms. They are *tsarah, akar,* and *ra.*

1. *Tsarah* is the most frequently encountered word for trouble and means to "press" or "be squeezed into a narrow place." The idea of circumstances and/or people who put great pressure on you is uppermost. As I said, to be in trouble is to be under pressure, usually from others who demand some response.

4

2. *Akar* has in it the idea of stirring up so as to confuse, perplex, and cause distress. Added to that may be the presence of danger. The response demanded is hard to give and may contain considerable risk.

3. *Ra* is the term for what is evil, bad, and worthless. It refers to sin and its effects: adversity, affliction, calamity, and distress. Both good (*tob*) and peace (*shalom*) are contrasted with *ra*. This word demonstrates the close connection between sin and trouble.

In the New Testament there are also three principal terms for trouble: *thlipsis, tarache* and *skullo*.

1. *Thlipsis* means "affliction" and "tribulation" and, like *tsarah*, comes from a root that means "pressure." Here the idea is pressure exerted by rubbing one object against another. "Pressure" remains the root meaning of the term in modern Greek.

2. *Tarache* (verb, *tarasso*) means to "stir, stir up," "disturb," "rouse," and "provoke" and corresponds roughly to *akar*. However, whereas in *akar* the stirring leads to confusion or perplexity, in *tarache* it calls for action. The demand for a response is, perhaps, most prominent in this word.

3. *Skullo* means to "flay," "mangle," or "tear" and focuses largely on the effect a troublesome event is likely to have on someone.

Plainly, all of these terms point to trouble. Together they speak of an event of such a disturbing nature that it is likely to confuse a person, tear him

5

up, and pressure him to make a response at considerable risk.

There is no immunity to trouble in a world of sin. So, not only must you be unafraid to face trouble, but you must learn how God wants you to handle it when it comes. The likelihood is that you have rarely, if ever, had any biblical instruction in handling trouble, even though it is one of the most common occurrences in life. Unfortunately, few churches have adequately prepared their members for such matters.

This book fills that void. If trouble presses for a response, so be it! When you read and follow the directions in this book, you will be able to give a *Christian* response.

Do you know what God wants you to do when trouble comes? If you don't, then read on. In a world filled with trouble, you can't afford not to know.

1

PAUL'S TROUBLE AT ROME

Because there are so many passages that pertain to trouble, it would be impossible to cover them all in a book of this size. Therefore, I have chosen to focus on one passage and relate others to it in order to enlarge our perspective and clarify concepts as we go. That passage is Philippians 1:12-18:

> Now I want you to know, brothers, that what has happened to me has served rather to advance the good news, so that it has become evident to the entire Praetorian Guard, and to everyone else, that I am in bonds because of Christ. And most of the brothers in the Lord, gaining confidence by my bonds, have become far more daring in fearlessly speaking God's Word. Some, indeed, preach Christ out of envy and strife, but others out of good will. The latter are motivated by love, knowing that I have been placed here for the defense of the good news. The former proclaim Christ from a spirit of rivalry, not sincerely, thinking that they can add affliction to my bonds. So what! The key thing is that in every way, whether in pretense or in truth, Christ is proclaimed, and I am glad about it. And, as a matter of fact, I shall continue to be glad.

You must remember that when Paul wrote this letter to the Philippian church, he was in trouble; he was in prison in Rome. Soon he was to face the Roman Emperor Nero, that sly and vicious madman. Paul was not sure whether he would survive that encounter (1:19-25). But he was prepared for either outcome (1:20-24). What he wanted, above all else, was to give a successful witness for Christ —"that . . . Christ will be exalted in my body, whether I live or die" (1:20ᵇ) and "not be put to shame by anything" (1:20ᵃ). That is why he urged his readers to pray for a "provision given by the Spirit of Jesus Christ" (1:19ᵇ) that would result in his "deliverance" (1:19ᵃ) from all of the possible pitfalls in his encounter with Nero. Prison itself was troublesome, and the defense, before Nero, could be called nothing less. Both experiences made a stew of Paul's normal activities, placing him under the utmost pressure; and both demanded a biblical response from him. It is about such a response that he was thinking in Philippians 1:12-26.

But there is a difference between the two sources of trouble: one was present; the other was future. Paul had already had to face imprisonment and grapple with it. This he did successfully, as verses 12-18 clearly indicate. The trial before Nero was, however, yet to come; and Paul's mind was filled with anticipation of the opportunities and possible hardships ahead as he prepared for it.

These experiences have much to teach us, by both precept and example, about how God expects us to handle trouble. In this chapter I shall sketch the situation as Paul discloses it, and in the following chapters I shall attempt to draw out several of the principles involved in the two accounts.

WHAT HAPPENED TO PAUL

Paul had appealed to the emperor and been sent to Rome to stand trial. We leave him awaiting that trial as the Book of Acts closes:

> And he stayed there for two full years in his own rented quarters and welcomed everybody who came to see him. He preached God's empire and taught about the Lord Jesus Christ with great boldness and without hindrance (Acts 28:30, 31).

In those verses we see Paul accorded much freedom. But when we open the Book of Philippians, it appears that a new development has taken place: Paul is in chains (1:13). Of course, it is possible that Paul was in chains during his house arrest, but that seems unlikely. It is easier to believe that matters took a turn for the worse beyond the close of Luke's account in Acts 28. In Acts, Paul seems to have enjoyed maximum freedom; in Philippians he seems to have been deprived of that freedom. That he was in chains is clear not only from Philippians 1:13, but also from Ephesians 6:20, where he alludes to the *alusis,* or coupling-chain, by which he was bound hand-to-hand to a soldier who guarded him day and night.[1]

That is how matters stood when Philippians was

1. Cf. Lightfoot on Philippians, p. 8.

written. Under such circumstances, many would grow resentful, while others would be found mucking around knee-deep in self-pity. Still others would strike out in anger, and some would be shattered.

Paul's response was different. In his answer to inquiries from the Philippian church, we discover his response:

> Now I want you to know, brothers, that what has happened to me has served rather to advance the good news (Phil. 1:12).

The word *rather* is intriguing. Paul begins a new subject when he writes, "Now I want you to know brothers . . ."; that is one of his favorite introductory phrases. Thus, after a salutation, a thanksgiving, and a prayer in the first 11 verses, the letter proper begins with verse 12. But how do you introduce a brand new topic with the word *rather,* a word of contrast? *Rather?* Rather than *what?*

No sense whatever can be made of this introductory *rather,* unless you presuppose a letter, or some message, from the Philippian church expressing a viewpoint to which Paul here, at the very outset, wishes to raise a forceful objection. "No," he is saying, "you have it all wrong. What happened to me served *rather* to *advance* the good news!"

While we do not know precisely what the Philippian church had said, we do know that they had looked on Paul's imprisonment (by now more than four years in all, including both the Palestinian and Roman stints) as a hindrance to the spread of the gospel. I can almost hear some of them talking: "Think of it: the greatest missionary of all has been shelved! Why? Has God goofed?"

Paul was interested in defending the honor of Christ and the wisdom of God. That is why, first crack out, he jumps in with all four feet to assert a contrary view, and he extensively defends it (vv. 12-27) by describing what God has already done to advance the gospel as the direct result of his imprisonment. He then mentions the great opportunity that lies immediately ahead.

HOW THE GOOD NEWS SPREAD

Paul's claim is that his Roman imprisonment already has served to *advance* the Good News. The Greek word translated "advance" (*prokope*) means to cut a way before one's self." It pictures someone hacking his way through underbrush, advancing by blazing a new trail. Paul is saying that his imprisonment, rather than curtailing the spread of the gospel, has enabled the Good News to cut into new territory that, otherwise, might have been untrackable. Then, in verses 13-18, he substantiates this claim by citing two clear-cut advances.

First, he mentions the evangelization of the Praetorian guard and the palace personnel:

> . . . so that it has become evident to the entire Praetorian Guard, and to everyone else, that I am in bonds because of Christ (Phil. 1:13).

Paul says that the gospel had become known among the entire group of 16,000 men who con-

11

stituted the Praetorian, or palace, guard! This guard was the emperor's own body of crack troops stationed at the palace in Rome. Paul says that the *entire corps,* and "everyone else" at the palace, had become aware of his presence and the reason for his imprisonment: ". . . that I am in bonds because of Christ" (13b). This was a remarkable outcome of Paul's imprisonment.[2] Just how did it come about?

We do not know the details, but we can certainly imagine what must have taken place without straying too far from the actual facts. When Paul was put into chains, coupled to guards, and restricted to a prison, he must have thought, "Aha! This is my opportunity. God has given me a captive audience." As various guards came and went on their shifts around the clock, and on various days, doubtless Paul presented the gospel to them. Some evidently came to faith in Christ. Paul worked carefully with these converts until they were well trained co-workers for Christ. As they went back to their fellow soldiers, they became missionaries to the palace guard and to others in attendance on the emperor. Thus the Word spread until Paul could say that "it has become evident to the entire Praetorian Guard,

2. Many of the men then in the Praetorian guard were later sent to France, Germany, and England (Gaul, Germania, Brittainia). It is they who may have first preached the gospel in these places to which, as far as we know, Paul himself was unable to travel. Thus, the imprisonment may have been the occasion for greater outreach than even Paul realized.

and to everyone else, that I am in bonds because of Christ." The result was that, from this gospel outreach, there were "saints" in "Caesar's household" (Phil. 4:22). It is important to understand Paul's argument because we shall have occasion to return to it again.

Paul's second proof that his imprisonment had advanced the gospel is found in verses 14-18:

> And most of the brothers in the Lord, gaining confidence by my bonds, have become far more daring in fearlessly speaking God's Word. Some, indeed, preach Christ out of envy and strife, but others out of good will. The latter are motivated by love, knowing that I have been placed here for the defense of the good news. The former proclaim Christ from a spirit of rivalry, not sincerely, thinking that they can add affliction to my bonds. So what! The key thing is that in every way, whether in pretense or in truth, Christ is proclaimed, and I am glad about it. And, as a matter of fact, I shall continue to be glad, . . .

Verse 14 sets forth the fact succinctly: "And most of the brothers in the Lord, gaining confidence by my bonds, have become far more daring in fearlessly speaking God's Word."

Because the travel of the greatest missionary in the world had been severely limited, and because there were so many opportunities and needs, a number of those who previously had thought, "Let Paul do it," or "There is no need for someone like me when Paul is out there to do the job," now began to reassess the situation. They reasoned, "Well, since Paul is no longer able to go here and there at will, someone else must go. I guess that means me!" So, brothers from all over began to come out of the woodwork; and the cause of missions throughout the Mediterranean world was actually boosted by Paul's imprisonment. Moreover, upon discovering how boldly Paul himself was proclaiming the Word within Caesar's palace, and with such good results, these preachers gained "confidence" and became "far more daring in fearlessly speaking God's Word" (v. 14). Thus, again, you can see how Paul's imprisonment "served *rather* to advance the good news" (v. 12).

Verses 15-18 are somewhat parenthetical and explain how some preached out of good motives while others took advantage of Paul's plight to advance their own interests. Either way, Paul says, "I am glad" that the gospel is being preached. He took no personal offense. He left those with improper motives for God to deal with; they were His servants, not Paul's. Clearly, he was following the pattern of his own admonition in Romans 14:4: "Who are you to judge somebody else's household servant? To his own lord he stands or falls. And he will stand since the Lord is able to make him stand."

WHAT PAUL LOOKED FORWARD TO

Now, thirdly, Paul looked forward with "eager expectation" to the opportunity of presenting the way of life to Nero at his defense. He wanted to exalt Christ by word and behavior in that hour (v. 20) and show a boldness throughout the proceedings that would command a hearing for what he had come to Rome to say. Tradition has it that he was eventually freed to carry on the "fruitful work" of which he speaks in verse 22 and to provide for the welfare of the churches about which he expresses concern in verses 24, 25.

So, throughout these verses, we encounter not a Paul who is passively languishing in prison, but an active, alert, working missionary who has carved out a new and exciting ministry in the midst of great trouble. Here is not a person who has given up, but one who is hard at the Lord's work and eagerly laying plans for new, ongoing ministries in the future. Paul was on top of his trouble.

While it may be going too far to say that Paul thrived on trouble, and he certainly did not believe in going out and stirring up trouble (I Thess. 4:11), nevertheless, it is a fact that he blossomed in it! Paul never minimized or underplayed the severity of persecution, suffering, or other kinds of trouble, but he always maximized the opportunities that trouble brought. In the chapters that follow I shall show you how you can do the same.

2

GOD IS IN THE TROUBLE

The most important fact to learn from what we have seen so far is that, above all else, *Paul saw God in his troubles*. He wrote, "I am in bonds because of Christ" (v. 13ᵇ). That is how God wants you to look at trouble too.

When trouble comes, many Christians react in ways that reflect the fundamentally non-Christian views still too much a part of their lives. Were you to ask them, in a purely academic setting, whether God is involved in their trouble, doubtless they would affirm He is. But when push comes to shove, and they are faced with a devastating trial of one sort or another, their working atheism (or, at best, deism[1]) rises to the surface. All of the rhetorical "whys," the bitter complaints, the hand-wringing self-pity, the seething anger, and the coming apart at the seams demonstrate a focus on self that effectively excludes God, at least for the moment.

Paul viewed trouble quite differently. His bonds, he declared, were not placed on his wrists by the Jews who accused him; nor did he con-

1. The view that God is not directly involved in what goes on in the world.

sider them Roman bonds. He wore the "bonds of Christ." And it was because Jesus Christ wanted him in bonds! That was the bottom line on trouble.[2]

Are you facing financial trouble, sickness, persecution, or some other hardship? If you must ask "why?," then don't make it rhetorical; hang around long enough to hear Paul's answer. You too will be able to reply resoundingly in truly biblical fashion, "I am in financial trouble (or sick or persecuted) because Christ wants me in this trouble." To be able to say this with the warmth of true faith is the first step in handling trouble God's way.

Now this viewpoint is rare—even among Christians; but Paul was a rare person. Here is one reason why: he responded to trouble as a Christian should! That is enough to make anyone stand out in this world of every other sort of response. His was a providential view of life: he saw God in the problem. And that makes all the difference. Trouble takes an entirely different perspective. It not only becomes endurable, but it begins to make sense—it takes on meaning and purpose. And as you will see in later chapters, this providential view opens new and different ways of handling trouble. That is why it is altogether necessary for you to understand and acquire such a view.

2. Cf. Eph. 3:1 where, similarly, Paul speaks of himself as the "prisoner of Christ."

ACKNOWLEDGING GOD'S PROVIDENCE
IN TROUBLE

What is providence, and how should it affect your view of trouble? In His working in history, God so sustains and governs all of His creatures and their thoughts and actions, as well as all events, that all of His gracious purposes are fulfilled, and yet in such a way that men remain wholly responsible for what they are, say, and do. That is providence. Providence means that God is actively at work in history, even those events we label "trouble." Such events are not hiatuses in God's providence, in which He turns His back and allows history to run its own course; they are a part of His active work, by which He brings to pass what ultimately will issue in His own glory and the blessing of His church. When all is said and done, there remain two—and only two— views of God in history: either (1) God goofs, or (2) God, in ways we don't now fully understand, providentially directs every phase of history (including trouble) toward His own good goals, which will be reached in His time and manner. Paul most emphatically opted for the latter view and, just as surely, flatly rejected the first.

Belief in God's providence will make an enormous difference in your attitude toward trouble, not to speak (yet) of how it will enable you to grapple with and gain mastery over it. While it is entirely proper to label trouble "trouble," it is altogether wrong to see it as *only* trouble. A providential view affirms that there is meaning and purpose to it, that, in fact, it is but a means to realize that purpose, even when your nose is pressed too tightly against trouble for you to discover its purpose. Belief that God providentially sustains and directs historical events is what makes it possible to follow Paul's directions to pray and give thanks rather than worry about trouble. Here is what he wrote in Philippians 4:6:

> Don't worry about anything, but instead in everything by prayer and petition with thanksgiving make your requests known to God, . . .

THANKSGIVING IN TROUBLE

"How can I give thanks for trouble? Prayer I can understand—but thanksgiving? Isn't that too much to expect?"

Yes, if you take the world's view; no, if you believe in God's providence. You will be able to give thanks if you truly believe that in spite of the misery and pain you may experience, He is in control of all things and does "all things well." It is a matter of faith.

"But surely, God doesn't expect me to give thanks when my son has just been run over by a drunken driver, or when my daughter has been raped by a sex pervert, does He? Am I supposed to go around with a smile on my face when my heart is breaking?"

No, I'm not asking you to deny your emotions their rightful expression. You will rightly sorrow, grieve, cry, become angry—or whatever else is biblically appropriate to the tragedy. It might be sin not to, particularly if yours is a callous, unloving attitude.

I am not saying that you should affect that nauseating, cavalier stance that some have adopted when, with a smile that impresses me as more of a stupid leer than anything else, they go around saying, "Praise the Lord, anyway!" There are people who would tell you, "My daughter just committed suicide; praise the Lord, anyway!" No, that's not what Paul is talking about in Philippians 4:6. Paul has no intention of stifling proper, God-given emotions. Christ Himself wept at the tomb of Lazarus (John 11:35, 36[3]) and elsewhere became angry at the Pharisees (Mark 3:5), in each case without sin. God does not want you to prance about like a laughing hyena in the face of serious trouble; not at all. He expects you to take sin and misery seriously. You must never minimize either.

"Well, then, what do I do?"

Just this: you are to thank God, even for the trouble that comes, *through* tears—not *instead* of tears. And you can do so if you know that, even when you cannot see how, God controls trouble, not allowing it to overwhelm you (I Cor. 10:12[4]),

3. The reaction of the Jews (v. 36) is revealing: "So the Jews said, 'Look at how He cared for him!' " Jesus' emotional response was an index of His love!

4. See my pamphlet, *Christ and Your Problems,* for an exposition of this verse.

He is working out His good purposes through it.

Such a view of life, I say, takes faith, of course; but faith is what Christians are called to exercise. Your Christian life began in faith; it must continue in faith; and it will be completed in faith. Faith sees what the eye can't see; faith understands what the mind cannot fully work out. At times, faith may speak this way, "I don't feel like thanking God, I don't see anything good in this trouble, and I hardly know the words to say; but I do believe the Scriptures, I do want to please God in all things, and so, Lord, I thank you—even for this." To give thanks in trouble it is not necessary for you to become a masochist who revels in pain, sorrow, and grief. Rather, God wants you to be thankful for the purposes He is bringing about—not for the sorrow and pain themselves. Thus David can write: "It is good for me that I was afflicted, so that I may learn Thy statutes," and, "Before I was afflicted, I went astray; but now I keep Thy saying"[5] (Ps. 119:71, 67, Berkeley).

5. Even self-induced trouble, or trouble sent remedially can be received with thanksgiving for its salutary effects. Cf. II Cor. 7:8-11: "Even if I caused you pain by my letter, I am not sorry for it (though indeed I was sorry). I see that you were caused pain by that letter for a short time, but I am now delighted—not that you were pained, but that your pain led to repentance. You were caused pain by God that you might in no way suffer loss by us. Pain that comes from God produces a repentance leading to salvation that no one needs to be sorry about. But pain that comes from the world produces death. Now, just look at the earnestness that this pain from God has produced in you; what a desire to defend

21

Here, the word for affliction is general and could apply to any and all sorts of trouble. Notice, the psalmist's eye is not on the pain but what it produced. He is virtually saying, "The suffering was worth it for what came out of it."

It is this rational, purposeful element the Scriptures introduce into the milieu of trouble that enables you to endure, find meaning in, and face trouble with a confidence and certainty that only a Christian who relies on God's promises could experience.

Probably, then, the most basic factor in handling trouble God's way is a correct viewpoint—one in which you see Christ in your problem. Whether you have that viewpoint will determine your fundamental stance toward trouble, which, in turn, will affect your attitudes and all of your actions. When hard times come and persist, and you feel as though you were chained to a problem, unable to move, you will know that your chains are the bonds of Christ. Every believer who ever achieved anything for Him suffered—and took this viewpoint toward trouble (see Gen. 50:20; Heb. 11:24-26, 35[b]). If you want to serve Christ well in trouble, you too must have the same viewpoint; there is no other way to do so.

What is your trouble? Write it out:[6] The trouble

yourselves, what indignation, what fear, what longing, what enthusiasm, what concern for justice! In every way you have proved yourselves to be innocent in the issue."

6. Often it is important to define trouble more clearly; sometimes our suffering, at least in part, grows out of uncertainty and confusion.

that I am facing at present is _the cleaning_

and sale of my home and

deciding where is best to

move I'm 84 years old

Now, having written that down, read the following out loud and believe it:

GOD IS IN THAT PROBLEM.[7]

and finding where is
best to move in the short
run as living in the
daily hope of thing
becoming better in the United
States and living as God
would have me live
for my remaining days on
earth before living with
God God Forever.

7.   Return to this page as often as necessary and reread the
last few sentences, filling in whatever problem you may be
facing at the moment.

3

GOD IS UP TO SOMETHING

As important as it may be for you to put God into the picture,[1] that is only a beginning. To handle trouble biblically, you must also recognize that trouble is a sign that God is up to something. It does little good to see God in the trouble if you view Him as passive. God is *actively doing* something; that trouble has a purpose. That is what Joseph meant when he declared, "True enough you planned evil against me, but God planned[2] it for good,[3] to bring about what today is fact, the keeping alive of much people" (Gen. 50:20, Berkeley).

Notice carefully in that great declaration of faith and understanding that the very same trouble (selling Joseph into Egypt)—with all of the troubles that followed—was calculated by man and by God to produce entirely different results. Truly, man proposes but God disposes. So you have a

1. Actually, God is there all the time as the subject of the picture, its background, its foreground, etc. He is all in all. We do not "put" Him into the picture; what we do is put Him into the picture for *ourselves* and *others*. That is to say, we recognize and acknowledge that He is there. It is that recognition and acknowledgement that is basic.

2. In both phrases the word translated "planned" means to intend or think to do something.

3. The words "good" and "evil" are *tob* and *ra*. *Ra* is one of the words for trouble.

choice; you may concentrate on what man is doing or on what God is doing in the trouble. And what a difference it makes whether you focus on what God is up to or what man is up to!

Whenever trouble comes, it is important, then, to ask yourself not only what others are up to (i.e., planning and doing), but what God is up to (planning and doing). Notice too how Joseph sees the ultimate purpose behind all of his hardship and suffering. It was larger than the blessings and benefits he personally received; he saw his trouble as the way God intended to bring about the survival of many people! Doubtless, earlier he began to see some of the personal blessings that God also intended for him. These brought meaning and purpose into his trials. But later on, he began to realize that God was up to much more; there was a purpose in Joseph's trouble that extended to others. Joseph began to see himself as a man of destiny.

You too are a person with a destiny; much more is happening when trouble comes your way than you will understand for some time to come. Believe it, and be on the lookout for it so that some day, when the outcome of the trouble has developed to its full, you will not fail to recognize it.

All who have done things for Christ that count have known these three truths and lived by them:
1. God is in the trouble.
2. God is up to something in the trouble.
3. God is up to something that will affect both me and others—perhaps many others.

25

All believers are men of destiny. In the body of Christ the arm is no more important than the little toe. As a part of that body, what happens to one happens to all. In a later chapter, you will learn more specifically how others are affected by your responses to trouble. For now, let us concentrate on another matter.

If you say to yourself when trouble comes, "God is up to something," the next question for you to ask is, "Hmm, I wonder *what* God is up to?" If you truly believe God is in the trouble and is doing something through it, your attention will be drawn away from the trouble itself and from those aspects that would lead to resentment or self-pity. Instead, your deepest concern will be to find God at work. When trouble appears, you will view it, among other things, as a sign of God's activity in your life.

Now, as I have observed already, you will not always be able to discern God's good hand immediately when trouble assaults you; your nose may be too tightly pressed against the brick wall. But even then, just as you can give thanks because by faith you know God is at work, you can ask God to help you grasp, as soon as possible, some threads by which you may begin to unravel the mystery of His providence.

Surely, as we have seen, Joseph's full conclusion, so beautifully expressed in Genesis 50:20, was only after a considerable amount of thread-pulling over a long period of time. But that conclusion would *never* have been reached had he not been the sort of person who, all along, knew that God was up to something, and had he not gone thread-hunting.

Bit by bit, piece by piece (to change the figure) Joseph put the puzzle together. But he wouldn't even have started to find the border pieces, had he not been aware that meaning could be brought out of the scrambling of colors found on these scattered pieces. In this life, of course, you will never finish the puzzle. But you can go far enough with it to discover patterns of providence, as Joseph did, and some of the purposes God had in mind. Even Joseph didn't know about the blessings that the biblical account of his troubles, including his great statement in Genesis 50:20, would be to all generations to come. Thus, we today can discover even more of God's purpose in Joseph's trouble than Joseph himself did.

Turning again to Paul's account in Philippians 1, we find a response very similar to Joseph's. When Paul was incarcerated, he too must have thought (perhaps even recalling the story of Joseph), "God is up to something; I wonder what?" Knowing that he had been set apart for a ministry of the Word (II Cor. 4:1), he must first have asked, "How does God intend to use me as a gospel preacher here?" As we have learned, there were many opportunities on the horizon, if he would only lift his eyes to see them. Others might hang their heads in self-pity and miss them altogether. But not Paul. He lifted his eyes all right. He virtually strained his eyesight trying to see as far into the future as he could!

Acts 28:17-31 shows his early response:

> After three days he called together to him the
> Jewish leaders, and when they had gathered,
> he said to them, "Brothers, although I have
> done nothing against my people or the cus-
> toms of our fathers, I was handed over as
> a prisoner into the hands of Romans, who,
> when they had examined me, wanted to free
> me, because there was no ground for putting
> me to death. But when the Jews protested, I
> was forced to appeal to Caesar, although I
> didn't have any charge to bring against my
> nation. For this reason I have asked to see you
> and speak to you, since it is because of Israel's
> hope that I am bound with this chain." And
> they said to him, "We haven't received any
> letters from Judea about you, nor has any of
> the brothers coming here reported or said
> anything bad about you. But we think that it is
> right to hear from you yourself what your
> views are, since we know that people every-
> where are talking about this sect." When they
> had arranged for a day to meet with him, they
> came to his lodging in large numbers. And he
> explained the matter to them, testifying about
> God's empire and trying to persuade them
> about Jesus from the Law and the Prophets,
> from morning till evening. Some were con-
> vinced by what he said; others disbelieved.
> Since they were in disagreement with one
> another, they left after Paul had spoken one
> parting word: "The Holy Spirt was right when
> He said to your fathers through the prophet
> Isaiah, 'Go to this people and say, You will
> hear and hear, but you won't ever under-
> stand; you will look and look, but you won't

ever see. This people's heart has grown thick, and their ears have become hard of hearing, and they have closed their eyes lest they might see with their eyes or hear with their ears, or understand with their heart and turn, and I shall heal them.' Let it be known to you, then, that this salvation from God has been sent to the Gentiles—and they will listen." And he stayed there for two full years in his own rented quarters and welcomed everybody who came to see him. He preached God's empire and taught about the Lord Jesus Christ with great boldness and without hindrance.

Those opportunities seem, however, to have grown less frequent. The Jews largely rejected the message (they were already divided by the gospel; cf. 28:24-28), and as I noted, Paul might have been transferred to a prison by the time the Book of Philippians was written. At each point, however, it is important to observe that Paul looked for the opportunities God was affording to preach the gospel. Almost as an assumption, Paul must have concluded, "Whatever else God is up to, surely He is providing new occasions for preaching Christ." So he watched for them. You can discern the first development of this pattern already becoming apparent in the last chapter of Acts.

But then, at some point, the change occurred. Paul was sent to prison. Guards were stationed much more closely to him, and he must have pondered, "Well, since my troubles are increasing, so must my opportunities be increasing too."

Thus, he began a new search for God's handiwork in the trouble. You can picture any number of ways in which it might have happened. Consider the following as one possibility:

Guard: "Your name is Paul?"

Paul: "Yes."

G.: "I hear you are some kind of Jewish zealot or something."

P.: "I'm a Christian, a preacher of good news."

G.: "Yeah? Well, just what is a Christian, and what is this good news? Tell me about it; we've got plenty of time on our hands."

P.: "Well, you see. . . ."

And off it goes—the beginning of Paul's mission to the palace at Rome!

Little by little things became clearer. Little by little the mission expanded into a marvelous ministry. The more Paul faithfully worked with each guard, the more guards were saved, instructed, and trained; and the more his ministry grew among the soldiers and others in Caesar's household. All along, what God was up to came into clearer and still clearer focus. Faithful recognition and pursuit of God's purposes in smaller ministries led to larger ones. That is nearly always God's order: "Whoever is trustworthy about smaller things is trustworthy about larger ones, but the one who is dishonest about smaller things is dishonest about larger ones" (Luke 16:10).

At any rate, Paul would never have had a ministry reaching to the entire 16,000-man body called the Praetorian guard, and to others in the palace, had he not seen God in the trouble, known that God was up to something in the trouble, and searched until he found those places where God was actively at work. First, he entered into those opportunities provided by the relative freedom of living in rented quarters. Next he made the most of the advantages of a more restricted environment.[4] And, as he writes, we encounter him "eagerly" anticipating what lies immediately ahead. But that isn't all—we read also of tentative plans for ministering to the churches, if he should be released by Nero.

Like Joseph, Paul was a man whose beliefs affected his life. He believed deeply enough to find God in the trouble and respond to the implications of what he found.

Do you believe that God is in your trouble, Christian? Will you then lift your eyes to the horizon? Begin by searching out those ways in which God may be giving you increased opportunities for doing whatever He has called you to do for Him in life. Start small, but think big. What you find at first will not exhaust God's purposes. As you pursue God's hand at work, still greater purposes will emerge. Don't stop at the beginning; patiently, gradually pursue all that God is up to until, with Joseph, you can reach off into the distant horizon where the goodness of God's plan becomes evident. Prayerfully consider your trouble this way. Then list below how your present

4. Yes, I said "advantage." Every circumstance has advantages peculiar to it, if we only have eyes to see them!

trouble may afford increased, or at least new, ways of pursuing your work for Him.

WAYS GOD MAY BE AT WORK

1. _____

2. _____

3. _____

4. _____

5. _____

6. _____

7. _____

8. _____

9. _____

10. _____

4

GOD IS UP TO SOMETHING GOOD

"But God planned it for good" (Gen. 50:20). Joseph said it; Paul repeated it: "God makes everything work together for the good of those who love Him . . ." (Rom. 8:28); and in times of trouble you must affirm this truth too. Otherwise, when trouble comes, you will find yourself bringing shame upon the name of Christ.

When you believe this great truth, with Paul, you too can rejoice, sing hymns, and give praises to God in the midst of trouble. In the Philippian congregation, there was a jailer who knew that Paul's words in chapters 1 and 4 (e.g., "rejoice in the Lord always") were not the words of an ivory-towered academe who had never put truth into practice; he, himself, had seen Paul in action:

> But when her owners saw that their way of making money for the future was gone, they grabbed Paul and Silas and dragged them to the marketplace to the rulers. When they had brought them before the chief magistrates, they said, "These persons are Jews and are causing our city a lot of trouble. They are advocating customs that it isn't lawful for us Romans to receive or practice." The crowd joined in attacking them, and the magistrates tore off their clothes and ordered them to be

33

beaten. After many stripes had been laid on them, they threw them into prison, ordering the jailer to keep them securely. So when he received this sort of charge, he threw them into the inner prison and secured their feet in the stocks. But about midnight Paul and Silas were praying and singing hymns to God, and the prisoners were listening to them, when suddenly the ground shook so violently that the jail's foundations quivered, and all at once all the doors swung open and all the chains fell apart. When the jailer awakened, he saw that the doors of the prison were open and had drawn his sword and was about to kill himself, because he thought the prisoners had escaped. But Paul shouted out, "Don't harm yourself! We're all here!" He asked for lights, rushed in and, trembling with fear, he fell before Paul and Silas. Then he led them out and said, "Sirs, what must I do to be saved?" And they said, "Believe on the Lord Jesus and you will be saved, you and your household." So they told him God's message, along with all those who were in his household. And he took them in that very hour of the night and washed their stripes, and he and all his family were baptized right away. Then he brought them to his house and made a meal for them and, together with his whole household, rejoiced that he had believed in God (Acts 16:19-34).

Not only is it important to locate God in the trouble and to recognize that He is up to something, but it is every bit as vital to affirm that what He is doing is good. Otherwise, there may be much understanding and yet little hope. Joseph and Paul said God's providence is *good*. You must believe this wonderful truth; after all, it is a great mercy of God that He has revealed the fact. Had He not, you might never have bothered to look for God's presence in the problem, and you too would be doomed to the pagan point of view on life. You would be unable to handle trouble. Life would become a total tragedy, not at all worth living. But the statement is true! And you must affirm its truth—even when not enough time has elapsed yet to see it demonstrated: *God is up to something good for His children.* Yes, even that tragic death, or rape, in more ways than you could ever track down in this life, is intended by God for the good of many.

God, of course, does carefully qualify the promise, when He appends the all-important words, ". . . for the good of those who love Him, for those who are called according to His purpose" (Rom. 8:28[b]). To unbelievers, He has made no such promise. Although He may bring calamity, or the threat of it, upon unbelievers to bring them mercifully to repentance (cf. the Book of Jonah), He gives no assurance that trouble will work out for the good of non-Christians. Indeed, the Bible teaches the opposite; there is no hope of a good outcome to those who persist in their sin and unbelief. And, ultimately, rather than experiencing the greatest good of all, eternal freedom from sin in the presence of God, they will be cast into the everlasting troubles of hell.

"But how could the rape of a child turn out for her good, and the good of many others?"

The specific answer to that question will vary from person to person and situation to situation, but in each case there is an answer to be found. Also, it is important to remember that the purposes of God take time to work out. They gradually come into view as God works them out one by one, as you gain perspective on them, *and* as, in *faith*, you look for meaning. The problem with people who seem never to be able to comprehend how tragedy can work for good is that they don't have faith to believe it. Not having such faith, they seek no answers or seek wrongly or give up too soon. The person with faith is firm, even in such circumstances. He does not give in to doubt. Because he believes, he searches until he finds. First, there are initial indications that God is at work; then, more and more, it plainly appears how God is making "the wrath of man to praise Him" by bringing good out of evil.

Unbelievers will not accept this reasoning. They have no faith in the promises of God in Scripture. But God expects you, a believer in Jesus Christ, to think and act in faith.

A rape *is* a tragedy. In itself, there is nothing good that can be said about it. But when it affects a Christian, it is not "in itself"; God is in the problem, and He is up to something good. But because it so greatly upsets a woman's present course of life, causing her to think seriously about her life and the world in which she must live, and because it screams aloud for a thorough reevaluation of the

36

purpose and place of sexuality,[1] there are obvious immediate benefits, if she is willing to pursue them. She must, of course, have a biblical stance, or she will not do so. At the very least, such a tragedy can cause a woman to grow beyond her days in Christian faith and maturity. How she handles her trouble will be a witness, or lack of it, to unbelievers. And the occurrence clearly provides opportunity for the church to minister to the rape victim and receive, as well as share, the blessings of a caring ministry. In the end, rightly handled, her trouble should bring her closer to God and to other members of His family.

Such general observations can be understood even before any special benefits pertaining to the peculiar circumstances of an individual's situation could be discerned. In other words, it is always possible for the believer who is prepared to do so to learn something significant from tragedy—to grow. That, then, is the place to start the search for purpose and meaning, if nothing specific is immediately apparent.

Joni Eareckson is an excellent example of someone who searched the rubble of her shattered life and found that God was at work among the pieces, giving her a ministry that otherwise would never have been possible. Her story, in film and book, also indicates that it took time for more and more of the ramifications of what good things God had in

---

1. A truly biblical counselor could help her think through all of these matters.

mind to appear; they cannot all be found at once. Impatient persons, with little faith and hope, will give up too soon.

But, what are some other good things that may flow from trouble? I have already mentioned Psalm 119:71, 67: "It is good for me that I was afflicted, so that I may learn Thy statutes," and, "Before I was afflicted, I went astray; but now I keep Thy saying" (Berkeley). In Psalm 119:71, the writer plainly states that affliction (trouble) was the occasion for a change of lifestyle. It broke the logjam. Prior to his trouble, he confesses, "I went astray." However, after trouble had its full effect, he declares, "but now I keep Thy statutes." Trouble does not always have such an effect on people, even God's people. Whether or not it will for you depends largely on whether you turn to the Bible for instruction and assistance, and whether you claim the promises found in it and follow its directions. The Bible performs no magic; you must approach and follow the Scriptures prayerfully, asking God's Spirit for wisdom to enable you to understand and for power to do God's will. Surely, when you do, this in itself will so deepen your own understanding of life and enhance your growth in Christian behavior that, if no other benefits arise from the tragedy, these alone would make it all worthwhile.

But, as we have seen, there are more. Remember, I have been able to mention only some of those general benefits that every believer may extract from trouble, no matter what the particulars of his situation may be. The special blessings, growing out of the particular features of the circumstance, are often the most profound of all; look at Paul and Joseph and you can see that. They put almost all of the emphasis on them. But since I know nothing of your own circumstances, I can only urge you to search for God's special benefits in them.

Let me mention just two more general blessings:

From James 1:3 we learn that "the testing of your faith works endurance." Endurance is a valuable commodity owned by all too few. Endurance is needed to succeed in every endeavor. It is the ability to hang in there when the going gets tough. Trouble is, among other things, an exercise in enduring pressure. Surely you could use more endurance, couldn't you? Well, that may be one reason why trouble is headed your way.

The last general benefit I shall note is the good that trouble may do to promote your ministry to others. In Joseph's case, not only did his suffering save a nation from starvation; it led to the repentance of his family.

While there is no reason for you to rejoice in trouble itself, certainly you can agree that in its results there is much to be thankful for. You can begin to see some daylight in the midst of the forest, can't you? Well, there is yet more to come.

But even now, as you begin to size up trouble the way Paul and Joseph did, as you begin to see God in the trouble working good things, can't you, with Paul, begin to get even a little bit excited about the potential power of trouble handled rightly? Think of it! Excitement in the midst of trouble! Would you have believed it possible before you began to view things God's way?

Using the list at the conclusion of the previous chapter, try to think of some good outcomes that might issue from the ways you have discovered God at work.

5

YOU MUST GET INVOLVED

If, as we have seen, there is meaning and ministry in trouble and good to be realized, then surely you do not want to miss out on it. But exactly how can you be sure to get the full benefit out of trouble?

So far we have seen that you must adopt the biblical viewpoint that trouble has meaning, you must search out what God is up to, and you must recognize the good that may flow from His providential governing of all things. But that is not all. In addition, you must get involved in what you see God doing through trouble.

That is what Paul did. When he found that God had provided a rented house, he turned it into an auditorium for proclaiming Christ. When that privilege was taken away, and he was moved to a prison, he viewed that change as a new phase in God's activity and joined in. God, he recognized, had thrown him into a closer relationship to the Praetorian guard. His chain was a chain by which Christ was leading him to a new ministry. He did not resist it, but followed the chain to the opportunities to which it was linked.

41

Unlike others, you must not overlook the blessings in trouble by resisting God's work. Those who see nothing but the trouble itself, fuse and confuse the tragedy and God's providential ordering of affairs. So, naturally, they resist what God is doing because they see nothing more than trouble itself. They see nothing but a chain, not a link with God's providence. On the other end of that chain, they see but a soldier, not a potential co-worker in the gospel. They see only a prison cell, not a seminary classroom. Because Paul believed God was up to something good, he saw more than a chain, a soldier, and a cell. He saw God at work in the trouble and joined in. You too must do the same.

"But how do I go about it?"

You must identify your chain and see what is on the other end of it. That's the place to begin.

"Give me a couple of examples, would you?"

Sure. There is a fire. All is destroyed: furniture, cherished items accumulated over many years, clothes, important papers and photographs—everything! That is a tragedy. The fire is a chain binding you to a great loss. There is no way out of the problem except by tracing the chain to its other end. There you will find God at work. In this case, you will find loss, irretrievable loss. Now what can you make of that?

If God is up to something good in the loss, the loss must not be viewed only as a tragedy but also as an opportunity. God has chained you to opportunity.

"But what opportunity can there be in loss?"

There are a number of possibilities. Let me mention several of them. First, such total loss can rip up roots that may have grown too deep. The fire may be God's way of freeing you from lesser things to greater service than ever before. Secondly, the loss will inevitably occasion great changes; but change provides opportunities to think and act differently in the future. Thirdly, loss can create a new flexibility and freedom of movement in terms of travel, change of location, even employment. I shall not develop this thought any further, although it would be possible to follow it up the street and around the turn.

"Well, I guess I could buy that, but how about another example? You said you'd mention a couple."

Certainly. Consider this: Your child is apprehended by the police for causing a very serious accident while driving under the influence of alcohol. The drinking, rebellious son is your chain (he's been a problem you've grappled with unsuccessfully for some time). That chain is now linked to a court trial involving a heavy fine and imprisonment, or both. Christ is in that problem. Believe it!

Perhaps the Lord has brought about this new development to make the boy rethink his lifestyle and his relationship to God. Rather than throw up your hands and shout, "This is the end!," as many parents would, you will wonder, "Is God about to change him? Could this really be a (costly) new beginning?" You know that in some way God is at work for good, and you will want to join in. Without nagging, you will confront your son with Christ in his new frame of mind, asking God to bless and to let you know through your son's response whether this is where He is at work.

The simple fact to remember is this: Wherever God is in the problem, you should be too!

Let me mention one other benefit. Even though it is more in the nature of a side effect, flowing from obedience to God, you may be able to see that failure to obey could occasion greater trouble of your own making, needlessly complicating matters. Taking God's route simplifies matters.

Often when serious trouble arises, demanding a decision and/or some other response from you, your immediate response is emotional. Energy is mobilized for action. That is not bad, as long as your energy remains under control and is properly used. However, whenever you do not know what course to follow, that energy is pent up and often multiplies in an upward cycle leading to panic. Even worse are the more frequent cases of impetuous action that is later regretted. Energy mobilized for action must be either subdued or channeled into constructive rather than destructive activities. The process of searching for and discovering God's providential hand in trouble, and then of deploying one's forces in work that grows out of the discovery, can soak up all the energy that otherwise might have been released in regrettable ways. The buildup of undirected energy is always dangerous. How important, then, it is for you to follow a biblically directed plan of action whenever trouble strikes! So, when trouble comes, your task is to find out what God is up to, and where He is at work, and then go to work beside Him.

6

EFFECTS OF BIBLICAL INVOLVEMENT

When you believe God is in the problem and is working for the good of His children, and you align yourself with Him by becoming biblically involved in as many of His activities as you are able to discover, you will find that certain inevitable results flow from such a course of action. I shall mention a few.

YOUR ATTITUDE WILL BE AFFECTED

Paul speaks of "boldness" (Phil. 1:20), "gladness" (v. 18), and "eager expectation" (v. 20). These are three highly desirable qualities, each of which is said to grow out of the viewpoint and course of action that Paul put into effect when he fell into trouble. By following him, you may begin to experience them too. You might expect the opposite effects to grow out of trouble. Many persons weaken and lose their confidence when trouble comes; boldness is as far from them as any attitude could be. Yet, that is exactly what is needed to face difficulties and enter into the opportunities that trouble brings. Boldness comes, in large measure, from knowing that God is in the trouble and that, therefore, you are not alone. Assurance that God is present and working good is the first element in boldness. Paul wanted to fearlessly make his defense before Nero; the way he went was calculated to prepare him to do so.

Again, gladness over God's action in trouble can overcome, or at least mitigate, the pain and sorrow that trouble brings. Isn't joy and gladness just what you need in trouble? Well, Paul was able to rejoice when he recognized how God had opened opportunities and used his trouble to encourage many others to fearlessly proclaim the gospel (v. 14).

And it is even possible to look forward to further trouble with eagerness, as Paul did (v. 20). When you become involved in what God is doing, trouble can become exciting and rewarding. Seeing the possibility of ministry in trouble changes everything.

It is equally true that if you do not take a biblical approach to trouble, that too will affect your attitudes. You are likely to become bitter, and you may slosh around in self-pity or swell with arrogance and pride. There are only two options: God's way or some other. Similarly, there are only two results: God-honoring attitudes or the opposite.

CHRIST WILL BE EXALTED

To exalt Christ in trouble was Paul's great desire (v. 20); to "be put to shame," i.e., to dishonor Christ, was his fear. That was why he wanted the "provision" of the Spirit as the result of the Philippians' prayers[1] (v. 19). You too will exalt Christ in trouble if you will do as Paul did and in humble boldness, depending upon the strength supplied by the Holy Spirit, will stand for what is right in God's sight.

Trouble will tempt you to compromise your stand for truth and righteousness and to take an easier way (that is the essence of Satan's third temptation of Christ). Paul could have avoided the confrontation with the Jews and the imprisonment in Rome if he had only adjusted his message. But he would not. To do so would be to shame rather than exalt Christ.

You must not compromise either. Be sure that your attitudes and actions exalt Him in trouble. That is the most important consideration of all. What ultimately does it matter if you are sad, if you experience pain and loss—even if you die? You are His; He is with you in it all, working good. What does matter is how others see Christ in you. While you may exalt Him by the way you witness in ordinary circumstances, there is perhaps no situation in which you may exalt Christ to unbelievers more clearly than when you handle trouble well.

YOU WILL ENCOURAGE OTHER BELIEVERS

The way Paul dealt with his imprisonment affected not only unbelievers but believers as well. They gained confidence from his example and

1. That is, the provision necessary for him to go through his defense successfully.

were encouraged to proclaim Christ fearlessly (v. 14). As always, some bad apples appeared in the barrel (vv. 15, 17), as they will today, but Paul would not allow them to deter, discourage, or divert him from his responsibilities. Personal affronts would not get him down or change his focus. He looked past all of that to the more important fact:

> The former proclaim Christ from a spirit of rivalry, not sincerely, thinking that they can add affliction to my bonds. So what! The key thing is that in every way, whether in pretense or in truth, Christ is proclaimed, and I am glad about it. And, as a matter of fact, I shall continue to be glad (Phil. 1:17, 18).

The "key thing" is what Paul kept before him always; his own welfare meant nothing by comparison. To become caught up in anything else is the always present danger. Don't let it happen. You will be able to avoid the danger only when, like Paul, you face trouble with concerns that are larger than yourself. Those concerns come from seeing God in the problem. Which leads to the last effect that I wish to mention:

YOU WILL ADVANCE THE GOOD NEWS

In every troublesome circumstance there is always an opportunity to advance the Good News in some way, directly (personal witness) or indirectly (encouraging others to do so). Paul's response to trouble did both. People watch you when you are in trouble, and the way you handle it may not only encourage and strengthen other Christians, but also exalt Christ before unbelievers, thereby providing a hearing for the gospel. This witness of your life may be followed by the witness of your lips.

God directs your concern away from yourself to others. (Read again the words of Joseph; reread Philippians 1.) What Paul said about himself related only to how his actions conditioned his witness to Christ. We learn nothing of the details of his suffering. His words are not the words of a self-centered person! In your present trouble, nothing could be more important than for you to turn your concerns away from yourself and to focus them on Christ. You will never advance the gospel until you do.

There are many other effects of a proper approach to trouble, but what I have mentioned should more than convince you that whether you respond well is not a private question or a matter of indifference. Much hangs on it, for good or ill.

7

PREPARE FOR TROUBLE

It is not always possible (or even desirable) to prepare for specific trouble; nor is it ever possible to prepare for every particular of that trouble. Jesus told His apostles that when they would be dragged before rulers they were to "Get it settled in your hearts not to practice your defense beforehand, because I will give you words and wisdom that none of your opponents will be able to withstand or contradict" (Luke 21:14, 15). And yet, even though Paul knew this fact, we see him (1) concerned about how he shall deport himself and (2) delighting in the Philippians' prayers for him as the source of his provision from the Spirit (19, 20). Though we hear nothing of his preparing a defense as such, in strict adherence to his Lord's explicit directions, nevertheless we do discover a genuine concern not to be "put to shame" (i.e., as Christ's ambassador to shame the One whom he represented). It seems safe to assume, therefore, that the promise in Luke 21 was not unconditional. Christ would supply His Spirit *in answer to prayer* (v. 19) and, presumably, not apart from it. Moreover, it seems possible that his behavior might cancel out the truth of his words. Otherwise, his concern over being "put to shame" seems pointless.

If Paul, having all the advantages of an apostle, was rightly apprehensive about his conduct in trouble and depended on the prayers of fellow believers to help him through the trial ahead (that is what "salvation" or "deliverance" means in v. 19), then, surely, you will need the same too.

Having the right viewpoint on trouble, searching out, finding, and joining God in bringing good out of trouble will mean little if you fail to ask God (often, like Paul, enlisting others' prayers as well), by His Spirit, to provide all that you need. Whatever you attempt in your own wisdom and strength will fail. Doubtless, it was a fear of such failure that occasioned Paul's concern. More than once he expressed a similar concern:

> And when I came to you brothers, I didn't come announcing the testimony of God in highflown speech or wisdom, because I determined to know nothing while I was among you except Jesus Christ and Him crucified. And I was with you in weakness and in fear and with much trembling. And I did not deliver my message or preach in persuasive words of wisdom, but with proof and power provided by the Spirit, so that you might not place your faith in human wisdom, but rather in God's power (I Cor. 2:1-5).

> Persevere in prayer, being alert in it with thanksgiving, praying at the same time also about us, that God may open for us a door for

the Word, to speak about the secret of Christ, because of which I am in bonds, so that I may proclaim it clearly, as I ought to (Col. 4:2-4).

He delivered us from so great a death, and He will continue to deliver us. He is the One on Whom we have set our hope that He will yet deliver us as you also cooperate by praying for us, so that many persons will give thanks for us because of the favor shown us in answer to many prayers (II Cor. 1:10, 11).

Who, then, among us dare plunge ahead on his own?

Preparation, for you and me, will involve thought about both what to say (we don't have the promise that was given to the apostles) and how to act. And both must be backed by prayer.

Studying the biblical principles of handling trouble and building a prayer network are the two most important preparatory measures that you can take. One thing is certain: you cannot avoid all trouble, no matter how hard you try; so prepare for trouble!

Once you understand well the basic outline of what you must do when trouble comes, and it has already become your pattern to respond accordingly, you will be free to focus on the particulars of each situation, giving them more careful attention than you could otherwise. Being thus prepared for trouble, you should (1) fear it less, (2) handle it better, and (3) honor Christ more consistently.

Just as the fear of fear, in the form of panic, becomes self-perpetuating, so may the fear of trouble intensify and thus produce more trouble.[1] It is very important, therefore, to know what to do beforehand.[2]

As a simulation, to help prepare you for trouble, think through how you would respond to the following situations. (If you are part of a class or a group studying trouble, you may wish to role play and discuss each.) In doing so, keep this basic outline in view.[3]

    A.   Recognize God is in the problem.
    B.   Remember God is up to something.
    C.   Believe that He is up to something good.
    D.   Discover where and how God is at work.
    E.   Get involved in what He is doing.
    F.   Expect good effects.

SITUATIONS
(for discussion and/or role play)

1. Your child has been run over by a drunken driver.
2. Your husband or wife has just left you.
3. You lose your job.
4. You are falsely accused of stealing.
5. You have an automobile accident.
6. Your house burns down.

1. For more on fear, see Jay Adams, *The Christian Counselor's Manual*, pp. 413-25.
2. Sometimes trouble is of a crisis nature. For more on crises, see "Coping with Counseling Crises" in my *Lectures on Counseling*.
3. It could be written out on a chalkboard for class discussion.

7. Your unmarried daughter becomes pregnant.
8. Your son is arrested for pushing drugs.
9. Your unsaved mother dies.
10. You lose everything you invested in the stockmarket.
11. Your basement floods.
12. You disagree with your new preacher on several basic issues.
13. Your church's youth program this year is very substandard.
14. You are not happy with the preaching in your church.
15. You are under pressure to change jobs.
16. You are having trouble selling your house.
17. Your automobile throws a rod.
18. Your doctor says you have cancer.
19. Your Ph.D. advisor doesn't like you.
20. Your application was turned down.

8

HANDLING SELF-INFLICTED TROUBLE

Whenever you bring trouble on yourself by your own sinful actions, there is an added element to consider. Everything else in the basic outline that I have given thus far remains the same but can hardly be operative until first you have dealt with your relationship to God and any others you may have wronged.

Obviously, you must repent of your sin:

1. Acknowledge and confess your sin to God and any others involved.
2. Seek forgiveness all around.
3. Rectify any wrongs that can be rectified.
4. Turn from your sin to biblical alternatives.

Sometimes, by following this biblical process, you will clear up the trouble altogether. Then, of course, the pressure will be removed, and you will be tempted to forget the other aspects of handling trouble that I outlined at the close of the previous chapter. Yet, to do that would be a great mistake.

God is no less involved in self-inflicted trouble, working for your good, advancing the gospel, and glorifying His Son, than He is in trouble coming from any other source. Nor does He expect you any the less to find your niche and become involved in what He is doing.

That God sends trouble to discipline sinning saints is attested, for instance, by I Corinthians 11:29-32:

> Whoever eats and drinks without discerning the body eats and drinks to his own judgment. It is because of this that many of you are weak and sick and a number sleep. Now if we carefully judged ourselves, we wouldn't be judged; but when the Lord judges us, He disciplines us so that we shall not be condemned along with the world.

Here sickness (cf. James 5:14-16[1]) and even death ("some sleep") are said to result from God's discipline. In the passage, God urges self-examination and self-judgment in order to avoid such trouble. Certainly, if nothing else may be gleaned from such an experience, you would want to discover how to avoid disciplinary affliction and trouble.

But you can and must do more than that. Sin brings shame and disgrace to the name of Christ. It is important not only to remove that shame by repentance, but also to bring good out of evil, and thus turn a defeat into a victory. God is in the

---

1. "Is anyone among you sick? Let him call for the elders of the church and let them pray for him, rubbing him with oil in the Name of the Lord, and the believing prayer will deliver the one who is sick, and the Lord will raise him up. And if he has committed sins, he will be forgiven. So confess your sins to one another and pray for one another so that you may be healed. The petition of a righteous person has very powerful effects."

business of transforming the defeat of crosses into the victory of crowns.

God, therefore, will work in the trouble you caused for yourself and others, to achieve goals that He has in view. In other words, He will be up to something good in which you may participate after genuine repentance, just as surely as though the trouble came upon you wholly from outside causes.

David's example is a clear instance of the biblical principle I am discussing. In Psalm 32 (and elsewhere) David publicly shared his own experience—humiliating as it must have been to do so—in order to warn, instruct, and help others. In this way, he turned a liability into an asset. In verse 8, he reveals a strong desire to see his tragedy become an aid to others. He says: "I will instruct you and train you in the way you shall go; I will counsel you with my eye on you."[2]

Often the trouble we bring on ourselves comes from other persons whom we wrong and who, in response, make waves for us. A wife may pout; a husband may blow his stack; a child may withdraw or become a behavior problem; a parent may place restrictions on a child. Two brief observations are in order in reference to these problems:

1. You must be sure that in seeking forgive-

---

2. For details on David's sin and repentance recorded in this psalm, Ps. 51, and Ps. 38, see pertinent passages in my book, *Competent to Counsel*. There is much more on sin and repentance in my books, *The Christian Counselor's Manual* and *More than Redemption*.

ness you do not mix accusations with confession. ("Please forgive me for saying those nasty things when you pulled that dirty deal," or, "Forgive me for what I did, and please stop being so rotten about it.")

2. Even after you have cleared up matters and forgiveness has been granted, the other party—particularly if he is an unbeliever—may not immediately stop the wave-making. If he is a believer, he may be confronted about this and be reminded that forgiveness is a promise not to raise the matter again.[3] With unbelievers, the matter may not be so simple. In such cases, Romans 12:18 comes into play:[4] "If possible, so far as it depends on you, be at peace with everybody." When the other person is still causing trouble, you will find that all six principles listed in the previous chapter are pertinent. You will not be so easily tempted to return evil for evil if you are energetically pursuing a biblical course of action in response to trouble. Retaliation is the direct result of a focus on self rather than a concern for the exaltation of Christ and the welfare of the other person.

So, the basic principles and procedures hold, even in cases where trouble is self-inflicted or sinful behavior calls down God's discipline, the negative responses of others, or both.

3. Ultimately, if he continues, the process in Matt. 18:15ff. may have to be activated.
4. For details on Rom. 12, see my book, *How to Overcome Evil*.

CONCLUSION

While much more could be said about trouble, and many other biblical passages and cases could have been studied and analyzed,[1] I have purposely decided against that approach. What you need is something short and solid that will form a basis for biblical decision and action. I have labored to provide just that.

May the great God, who assists us in all of our troubles, assist you with the same assistance that others have experienced. And may He be pleased to use this book in the process.

1. For classroom or group study, the principles of this book might be applied to a number of the cases found in *The Christian Counselor's Casebook*.